I0042588

# FOOD INSECURITY IN INFORMAL SETTLEMENTS IN LILONGWE, MALAWI

EMMANUEL CHILANGA, LIAM RILEY,
JULIANA NGWIRA, CHISOMO CHALINDA
AND LAMECK MASITALA

SERIES EDITOR: PROF. JONATHAN CRUSH

# ACKNOWLEDGEMENTS

The authors would like to thank the Social Sciences and Humanities Research Council of Canada (SSHRC) for its support of the Consuming Urban Poverty 2 (CUP 2) project.

AFSUN

© AFSUN 2017

Published by the African Food Security Urban Network (AFSUN)
African Centre for Cities, University of Cape Town, Private Bag X3
Rondebosch 7701, South Africa, and Balsillie School of International
Affairs, Waterloo, Canada
www.afsun.org

First published 2017

ISBN 978-1-920597-24-5

Cover photo: Sungwi market in Lilongwe by Emmanuel Chilanga

Production by Bronwen Dachs Muller, Cape Town

Printed by Print on Demand, Cape Town

# AUTHORS

Emmanuel Chilanga is a PhD Student, Centre for Research on Children and Families, School of Social Work, McGill University, Montreal, Canada, and Lecturer of Geography, University of Livingstonia, Livingstonia, Malawi

Liam Riley is a Postdoctoral Fellow at the Balsillie School of International Affairs, Wilfrid Laurier University, Waterloo, Canada

Juliana Ngwira is an Undergraduate Student in Public Health, University of Livingstonia, Livingstonia, Malawi

Chisomo Chalinda is an Undergraduate Student in Education, University of Livingstonia, Livingstonia, Malawi

Lameck Masitala is an Undergraduate Student in Education, University of Livingstonia, Livingstonia, Malawi

## Previous Publications in the AFSUN Series

# CONTENTS

# TABLES

# FIGURES

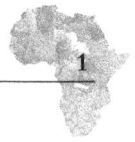

# 1. INTRODUCTION

Although there is widespread food availability in urban areas across the Global South, it is not correlated with universal access to adequate amounts of nutritious foods. In Southern Africa, empirical research has uncovered extensive food insecurity at the household scale in cities with an abundance of food.[1] An urban household food security baseline survey was administered by AFSUN in 2008 in a peri-urban community within the boundaries of Blantyre City which, due to its low population density and distance from the city centre, included many agricultural households.[2] In many other Southern African cities, the AFSUN research was conducted in informal settlements. As a result, Blantyre's findings appeared anomalous, with lower levels of food insecurity and much higher rates of participation in urban agriculture. However, most of Malawi's urban poor households reside in high-density informal settlements and, therefore, this type of urban environment needs to be surveyed to see if it conforms to broader regional patterns.[3]

This report is based on a household survey conducted in six low-income informal areas in Lilongwe, where three-quarters of the population live in informal settlements.[4] According to the former chief executive of the Lilongwe City Council, "the rapid population growth rate [4% per annum] is almost synonymous with the growth of informal settlements."[5] Understanding the dimensions of household food insecurity in these neighbourhoods is critical to sustainable and inclusive growth in Malawi's capital city.

The survey was conducted in July-September 2015 through a partnership between AFSUN, CUP2 (Consuming Urban Poverty) and the University of Livingstonia in Malawi. The report provides background information about Lilongwe and then discusses the research methodology. The following sections focus on household characteristics; food sources used by households in urban informal settlements and food purchasing patterns; and household food security in comparative perspective. The final section summarizes the findings, discusses public policy challenges, and makes recommendations for future food security research in urban Malawi.

# 2. URBANIZATION IN MALAWI

Malawi is one of the world's least urbanized countries, with only 15% of the population resident in urban areas at the time of the last census in 2008 (Table 1). Malawi's urbanization rate is also modest compared to other African countries, at 3.7-3.9% per year for the period 1998-2008.[6] The urbanization rate is suppressed by high rates of rural population growth, competing agricultural labour destinations as rural economic migrants move to other rural areas, migration out of the country especially to South Africa, and weak economic pull factors in the cities.[7] There are few formal sector employment opportunities to draw workers into Malawi's cities, and the high cost of living relative to incomes makes it difficult for households to sustain themselves in urban areas.[8] Moreover, there is a pervading ethos in government and among donors and international agencies that the country's development path should continue to be based on rural agricultural production.[9] As a result, there are few policies to address the growing problem of urban poverty.[10] Also, there is a high degree of circular migration between urban and rural areas, which means that many more Malawians are temporary urban residents than is suggested by census data.[11]

| TABLE 1: Urbanization in Malawi, 1966-2008 | | | |
|---|---|---|---|
| Year | National population | Urban population | % urban |
| 1966 | 4,039,583 | 260,000 | 6.0 |
| 1977 | 5,547,460 | 555,000 | 8.0 |
| 1987 | 7,988,507 | 857,391 | 10.7 |
| 1998 | 9,933,868 | 1,435,436 | 14.4 |
| 2008 | 13,029,498 | 1,881,010 | 15.3 |
| Source: Manda (2013) | | | |

The poverty in Malawi's urban areas is generally eclipsed by the country's extreme levels of rural poverty. A large majority of the population are smallholder farmers with little cash income.[12] Given the high degree of reliance on agriculture for the national economy and for the survival of most households, it is certainly understandable why urban issues have received less attention. Nevertheless, the specific issue of urban food security draws attention to the linkages between rural and urban households, economies, and development paths.[13] For example, urban consumers shape food market prices and demand for certain foods; urban workers play a key role in processing and trading agricultural commodities for export; and urban households provide cash remittances to relatives and

offer their homes to relatives seeking access to better educational and health facilities than rural communities can offer. Urban residents are also food producers, as many participate in agricultural production in town and in rural areas.[14]

There are two key reasons why it is prudent to pay more attention to urban trends in Malawi: first, there is the burgeoning demographic change of a very youthful population and, second, there are the growing challenges accompanying climate change. Table 2 shows the government's projections for population growth by age group, with a majority of the population under the age of 25 until at least 2038. As these young people seek to establish themselves on already crowded smallholder plots, we can anticipate increasing push factors off the land. Also, smallholder farming will become more challenging as climate change makes it more difficult to manage rain-fed agriculture.[15] Malawi's main food crop is maize, which is among the most sensitive crops to changes in rainfall patterns.[16] This creates a prospect of increased rural to urban migration just as national food production is destabilized by climate change.

Even with the predictable trends of population growth and climate change, it is difficult to envision how these processes will shape urbanization in Malawi. Some researchers argue that the urbanization process is oversimplified in much of the literature, which gives too little attention to the lack of reliable census data, the popularity of circular migration and temporary residence in African cities, and historical examples of de-urbanization.[17] One study in Malawi argues that climate change could lead to the decline of rural environmental resources and slow (or reverse) urbanization in Malawi in two ways: first, by depriving urban households of access to rural resources and making urban livelihoods untenable, leading urban residents to migrate to rural areas, and second, by reducing the capability of rural would-be migrants to move to urban areas.[18] This scenario does not account for possible changes in the urban and rural economies, which could make urban livelihoods less dependent on rural areas in the long run. Moreover, the growth of urban populations in Malawi is not only the result of migration; natural increase makes a large contribution to urban population growth and this population pressure will continue even if rural-to-urban migration slows due to climate change.

Malawi's overall urbanization trend is relatively low compared to most other countries, but its major cities including Lilongwe - the capital and largest city – are growing rapidly. Lilongwe's population is projected to more than treble in size from the 676,215 people recorded in the 2008 Census to 2,009,841 in 2028 (Figure 1).[19] One long-range model predicts that Lilongwe's growth will continue to accelerate beyond 2050, reaching

15,000,000 by 2075 and surpassing many of today's largest cities by 2100 with a population of over 40,000,000.[20] The suggestion that Lilongwe will continue to grow at the exponential rate needed to reach this population size is bewildering, given the current constraints on providing basic needs to its present urban population. And yet, the model's projections provide food for thought to development planners and research communities who continue to assume that Malawi's future will be rural.

### TABLE 2: Projected Population Growth and Age of Population, 2008-2038

| Population | 2008 (census) | 2018 (projection) | 2028 (projection) | 2038 (projection) |
|---|---|---|---|---|
|  | 13,102,076 | 17,931637 | 24,540,844 | 33,028,519 |
| Age groups | % | % | % | % |
| 0-14 | 46 | 46 | 44 | 41 |
| 15-24 | 20 | 20 | 20 | 20 |
| 25-49 | 25 | 26 | 27 | 28 |
| Over 50 | 9 | 8 | 9 | 10 |
| Source: Government of Malawi (c2010) | | | | |

### FIGURE 1: Population of Lilongwe City with Projections to 2028

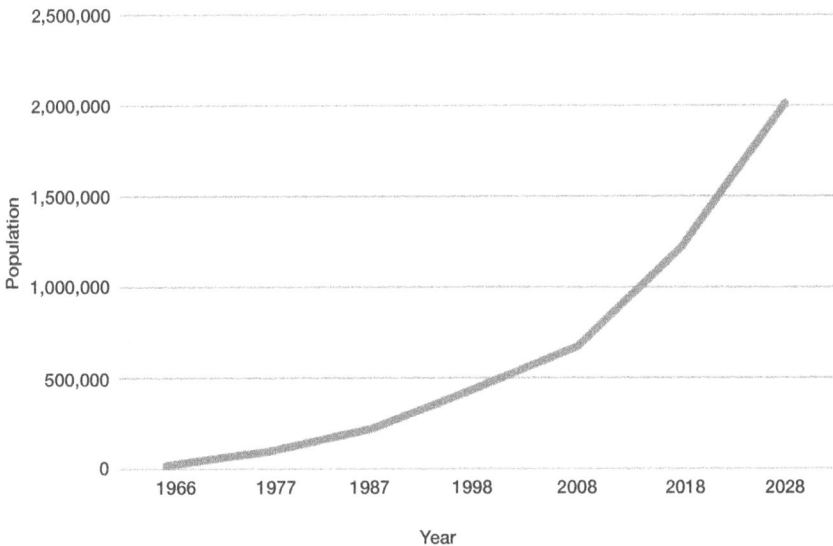

Source: Government of Malawi (c2010)

The current challenges with rapid informal growth can be partly attributed to Lilongwe's designation as the capital of Malawi in 1975. As with other capital cities built from a master plan, Lilongwe's planners did not account for the high rate of migration nor the high levels of poverty

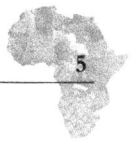

that would come to characterize the city.[21] Forty years after it became the capital, Lilongwe is characterized by a combination of low-density middle and upper-income neighbourhoods and high-density informal neighbourhoods that house most of the city's residents. The main market is located in the "old town" but several formal and informal food outlets cater to their respective constituencies of high and low-income consumers. The spatial legacy of the master plan for Lilongwe is a very dispersed urban area with concomitant mobility and transportation problems, particularly for low-income residents forced to live on the margins of the city and commute long distances for employment.

Widespread informality in Lilongwe has always presented challenges and these are likely to intensify with the projected population growth, coupled with environmental, economic, and demographic stress on the national food system. This report fills a major gap by providing recent empirical data on poverty and hunger in Lilongwe's informal settlements. It builds on and updates previous research that has shown the long-term structural nature of the problem of urban food insecurity in Malawi. This includes a 1988-1989 survey in low-income neighbourhoods in Blantyre and Lilongwe, which showed that three decades ago low-income households were already struggling to purchase sufficient food.[22] A more recent study of two "slum" communities in Lilongwe demonstrated in detail the ways in which HIV/AIDS, gender discrimination, and poverty shape food insecurity.[23] While the fact of hunger as a characteristic of urban poverty is therefore not a new finding in Lilongwe, this report provides further insights into the extent, depth and drivers of the problem.

# 3. METHODOLOGY

The study adopted a cross-sectional mixed methods approach including a household survey and associated qualitative research activities. The survey instrument was a modified version of the original AFSUN household food security baseline survey. It included sections on food security measurement, household economic activities, food sources, and other household characteristics.[24] The survey used the four FANTA measures of household food insecurity: the Household Food Insecurity Access Scale (HFIAS), Household Food Insecurity Access Prevalence (HFIAP), Household Dietary Diversity Score (HDDS), and Months of Adequate Household Food Provisioning (MAHFP). Combining these assessment tools adheres to the FAO-recommended approach that captures the multidimensionality of food insecurity, which includes day-to-day experiences of scarcity and hunger, lack of dietary diversity, and seasonal deprivation.[25] The survey also captures important data on food sources, food consumption patterns, and impediments to food access at the household scale.

Students from the University of Livingstonia administered the survey from July–September 2015. A cluster sampling technique was used to select six informal urban areas across Lilongwe (Figure 2). The research team then used systematic sampling to select participants in each informal settlement. Block leaders or chiefs provided names of households under their block and the research team randomly selected one household as a starting point. Enumerators then interviewed specific households according to the sampling interval in each block. The data was entered and cleaned by a team of Malawian and Canadian researchers.

**FIGURE 2: Location of Survey Sites in Lilongwe**

A total of 300 households were interviewed. Table 3 shows the areas that were sampled and the number of households interviewed in each. Areas 23 and 24 are located in the southeast corner of the city. Area 18 is centrally located and is one of the most densely populated areas in the city. Areas 25 and 50 are in the north of the city, with Area 25 at the northern edge. Twenty households were interviewed in Airwing, an area that developed informally around the old airport in the southwestern corner of the city.

| TABLE 3: Informal Neighbourhoods in Survey Sample | | |
|---|---|---|
| | No. | % |
| Area 24 | 60 | 20 |
| Area 25 | 50 | 17 |
| Area 18 | 100 | 33 |
| Area 50 | 30 | 10 |
| Airwing | 20 | 7 |
| Area 23 | 40 | 13 |
| Total | 300 | 100 |

Box 1 provides a picture of two neighbourhoods from the field notes of the student researchers: Ngwenya informal settlement in Area 24 and Mgona informal settlement in Area 25. These accounts depict a lack of infrastructure and the high cost of food relative to incomes.

## Box 1: Qualitative Observations of Study Sites

In Ngwenya, located in Area 24, Chisomo Khanyera observed a widespread lack of services, such as piped water and electricity, and generally poor-quality housing (including some houses built of sun-burnt bricks with grass-thatched roofs). There is little local employment and most people rely on piecework, known locally as ganyu, for their livelihoods. There are two markets in Ngwenya, one formal and one informal, and in addition there are many vendors operating outside of the markets. Locally produced foods such as vegetables, beans, and maize tend to be cheaper in Ngwenya than in nearby formal settlements, but processed foods such as oil, milk, and sugar are more expensive. Many migrants from rural areas live in Ngwenya. The researchers encountered particularly vulnerable children in Ngwenya. Many children who are being raised by their siblings or grandparents do not attend school and rely on charity for food. Residents also reported anecdotes of young girls engaging in sexual activities to access food from men.

In Mgona, located in Area 25, Juliana Ngwira found high unemployment and widespread poverty. She noted that new boreholes and access to piped water from the Lilongwe Water Board meant that water was available at a reasonable price, but food remained expensive. The price of whole maize was 850 Malawian kwacha (USD1.53) for a 5-litre bucket, which is extremely expensive considering that a 2013 report found that 46% of households in informal settlements had monthly incomes of less than 18,000 Malawian kwacha (USD32.38).[26]

# 4. HOUSEHOLD CHARACTERISTICS

The surveyed households were mostly male-headed (70%), with 27% female-headed and the remaining 3% headed by young people under the age of 18 (Figure 3). The majority of households had 4-6 members (67%), 21% had 7 or more, and 12% had 1-3 members (Figure 4). Respondents were asked to list all income sources for the household (Figure 5). Casual work and self-employment from informal businesses, which are highly precarious livelihoods, were reported as the most common income sources (64% and 36% of households respectively). Only 16% of households reported income from formal-sector wage work, which is reflective of the lack of formal-sector employment in Lilongwe, as well as the lack of access to secure employment in the informal settlements. Even with this precarious situation, the majority of households (81%) rely on only one or two income sources (Figure 6). Notably, no surveyed households received cash remittances from relatives. This is consistent with traditional patterns of fewer remittance-receiving households in urban areas and in the Central Region of Malawi.[27]

As many as 70% of the respondents said that the economic condition of their household was worse than it had been a year previously (Figure 7). A quarter (27%) said it was the same and only 3% said it was better. In 2015, the national economy was experiencing the effects of the Cashgate scandal that uncovered systemic theft from the public treasury and led to the withdrawal of budgetary aid, a slow-down in economic activity, and severe currency devaluation.[28] A key finding from the qualitative interviews conducted at the time of the survey was that many vulnerable residents linked their food insecurity directly to the effects of Cashgate on the local economy (including the availability of casual employment and informal business activities), the provisioning of public services, and the sharp increase in the cost of living.[29]

## FIGURE 3: Types of Households Surveyed

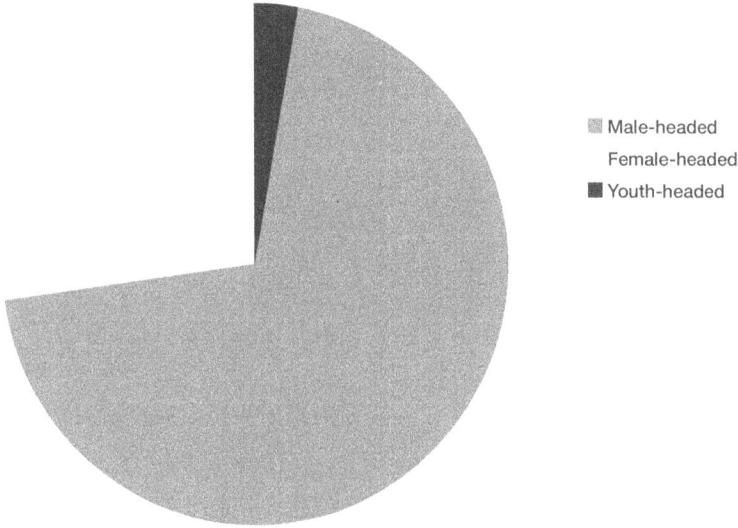

- Male-headed
- Female-headed
- Youth-headed

## FIGURE 4: Households by Number of Household Members

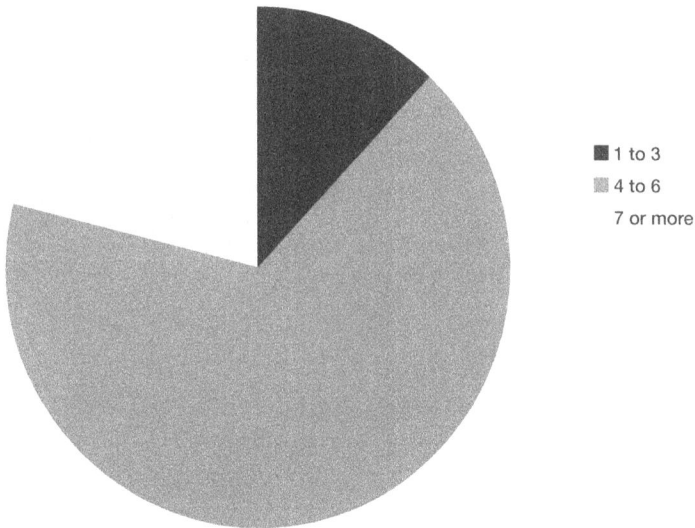

- 1 to 3
- 4 to 6
- 7 or more

## FIGURE 5: Sources of Household Income

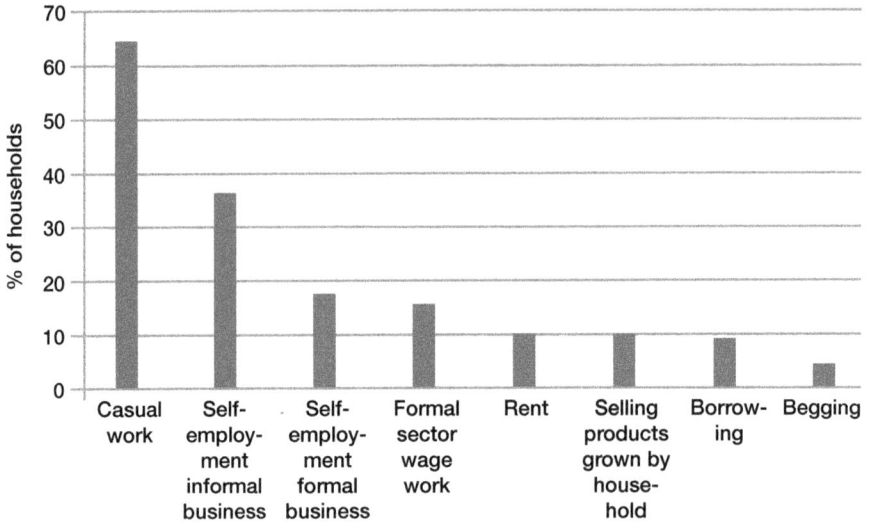

## FIGURE 6: Number of Household Income Sources

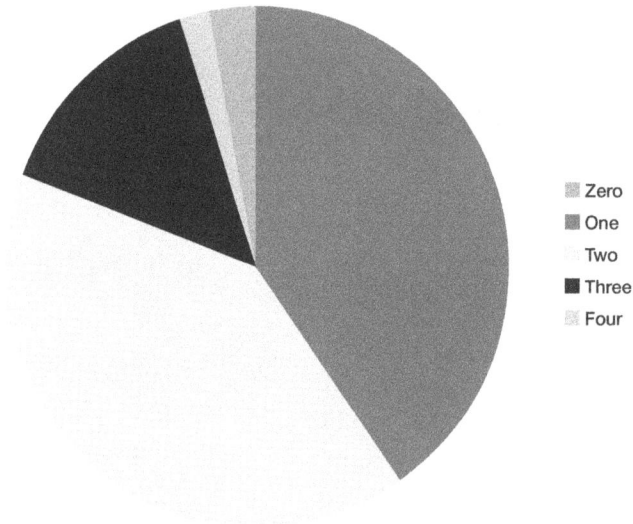

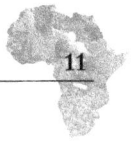

**FIGURE 7: Economic Condition of Household Compared to a Year Ago**

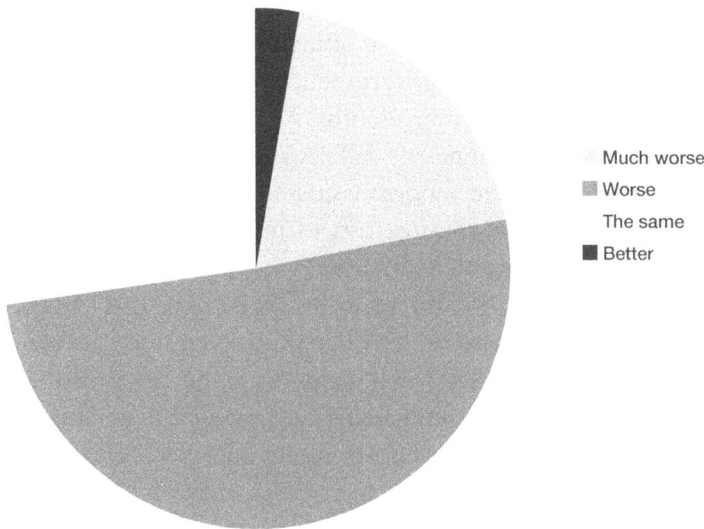

Much worse
Worse
The same
Better

The political and economic turmoil following Cashgate was compounded by 1-in-500-year floods in January 2015 that directly affected 15 districts and 1,101,364 people and had a national impact through interruptions to water, electricity and roads.[30] The floods were largely responsible for a 30% year-over-year decline in food production in the 2014/2015 agricultural season.[31] The floods were accompanied by late arrival of rains in some areas of Malawi, part of the increased frequency and intensity of droughts over the past four decades.[32] GDP growth had been strong in 2013 (6.3%) and 2014 (6.2%) but declined to 2.8% in 2015 "following the challenges of macroeconomic instability, late arrival of rains and the severe floods experienced in January 2015."[33]

# 5. FOOD SOURCES AND FOOD PURCHASING PATTERNS

The survey findings in Lilongwe are consistent with previous research in Southern Africa which has shown that households in low-income urban settlements rely primarily on purchasing from informal sources to access food.[34] Even in cities with high levels of supermarketization, informal vendors and supermarkets operate symbiotically, with consumers accessing food from both sources depending on their needs and resources.[35] In Lilongwe's informal settlements, informal and small-scale retailers dominate food provisioning. The tensions around formal and informal commercial activities in urban areas are a perennial feature of Malawian politics, dating back to the colonial laws governing urban commerce.[36] The first postcolonial regime under Hastings Kamuzu Banda (1964–1993) enforced strict regulation of the use of urban space and there were very few informal vendors. The first government elected under the multi-party system, led by Bakili Muluzi, identified with informal vendors and supported their economic interests.[37] This support included public investment in flea markets where vendors could conduct business.[38] The pendulum again swung against the interests of informal vendors under the subsequent president, Bingu wa Mutharika, who instituted Operation Dongosolo ("clean-up") in 2006 and again in 2011.[39] The 2011 events were particularly violent and tied to broader protests against the government's failed economic policies.[40] The national importance of these struggles indicates the scale of the informal sector, while the persistence of informal vendors despite decades of government efforts to curtail their activities reflects their central importance in the lives of urban Malawians.

In the context of Malawi, several of the food sources listed in Table 4 are at least partially informal. All of the surveyed households purchase food from street sellers/traders/hawkers (which includes informal market vendors) and small shops on at least a weekly basis (Table 4). Nearly half of the households purchase food almost daily (at least five days per week) from street sellers/traders/hawkers. "Small shops" and "fast food takeaway" are categories that include a variety of establishments that fall into "formal" and "informal" categories. In the context of the survey, "small shops" referred to shops in the neighbourhoods that are built using simple materials and tend to be temporary.

| TABLE 4: Household Food Sources and Frequency of Purchase | | | | | | |
|---|---|---|---|---|---|---|
| | At least five days per week | At least once per week | At least once per month | At least once in six months | At least once per year | Never |
| Street seller/trader/hawker | 45 | 55 | 0 | 0 | 0 | 0 |
| Small shops | 16 | 84 | 0 | 0 | 0 | 0 |
| Supermarket | 0 | 1 | 21 | 9 | 0 | 69 |
| Fast food takeaway | 0 | 0 | 22 | 26 | 10 | 43 |
| Restaurant | 0 | 0 | 2 | 3 | 1 | 93 |
| Growing food | 0 | 0 | 2 | 3 | 5 | 90 |
| Shared meals with neighbours | 0 | 0 | 0 | 6 | 16 | 78 |
| Borrow | 0 | 0 | 0 | 2 | 10 | 88 |
| From relatives | 0 | 0 | 0 | 0 | 3 | 97 |

At the formal end of the formal-informal spectrum of food sources are a variety of sources classified as supermarkets. The advent of supermarkets in cities of the Global South marks the acceleration and intensification of the integration of household food consumption into regional and global food supply chains.[41] This shift is associated with dietary shifts towards the consumption of more processed foods and the development of "food deserts" as local forms of food retailing become less important or are put out of business.[42] This process is highly contingent on local economic, geographical, political and cultural factors, and it is therefore important to situate the supermarketization narrative in local contexts.[43] Lilongwe has two Shoprite stores, which are South African-owned and represent the prototypical international chain brand supermarket. There are also several established domestic chains, such as People's, Metro and Chipiku stores, which have operated in Malawi for decades but do not typically offer the full variety of foods, consumer goods, and services found at Shoprite.[44] In 2014, People's was licenced to operate the South African SPAR brand and the first SPAR supermarket opened in Lilongwe in 2015.[45] There are, in addition, several boutique grocery stores catering to expatriates and wealthy Malawians, and several independent cash-and-carry stores.

In keeping with local nomenclature, supermarkets were identified in the survey as any food shop where an individual enters, picks products off shelves or out of refrigerators, and pays at the shop till. The category therefore includes outlets owned by multinational companies such as Shoprite and by individual business owners. Some large supermarkets owned by individuals (often of Burundian or Indian origin) are found in informal settlements. They provide cheaper food items compared to larger domestic and international supermarket chain stores. The qualitative follow-up interviews found that most people from informal settlements bought sugar and bread from the formal markets because the prices were more consistent than those of the small shops.

The survey found that 31% of households in Lilongwe's informal settlements purchase food at supermarkets, but most only do so on a monthly basis (Table 4). The low rate of supermarket patronage raises the question of why some choose to shop there and the majority do not. Figure 8 provides insights into the reasons why some people shop at supermarkets. The top two reasons given are the opportunity to buy in bulk and higher quality of produce. The utility of supermarkets is therefore the monthly provisioning of bulk supplies and groceries rather than the buying of daily consumables. A third of the households that patronize supermarkets disagreed that supermarket foods are cheaper.

**FIGURE 8: Reasons for Shopping at Supermarkets**

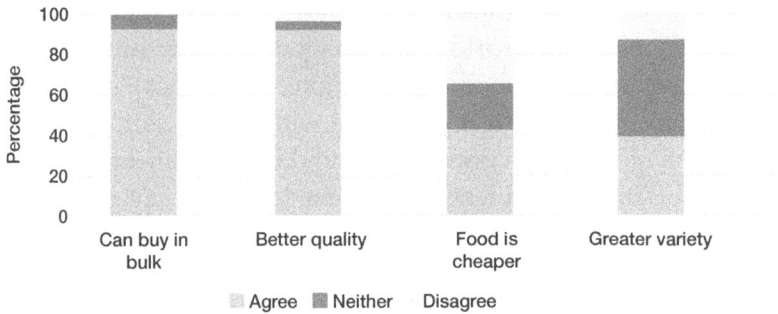

N= 103

The main reason for not shopping at supermarkets was that they do not provide credit (Figure 9). This is one area where informal markets and vendors have a competitive advantage. They often know their customers and are willing to make arrangements for late payments for food. Households that rely on precarious forms of income from casual labour and informal businesses experience inconsistency in the flow of cash income. When there is no money in the household, the availability of food on credit can make the difference between eating and not eating. Forty percent of respondents said that supermarkets were too far away. Few respondents agreed that they did not shop at supermarkets because they were only for the wealthy, too expensive, or did not sell the food they need. It is possible that a more restrictive definition of supermarket, referring specifically to Shoprite for example, would have yielded a higher percentage of positive responses to these questions. The findings suggest that if more supermarket outlets open near informal neighbourhoods, and if the companies find innovative ways to extend credit to customers in a largely unbanked society, then rates of supermarket patronage will begin to increase.

Table 5 shows how many households purchased each food item from a list included in the questionnaire and the frequency with which these foods were purchased. The majority of households had not purchased bread (72%) or fresh milk (74%) in the previous month. This does not necessarily indicate food insecurity per se because bread and milk are not part of the traditional rural diet. However, they are associated with urban diets in Malawi and are widely available, so their absence could be interpreted as a sign of constrained food budgets. The impression that people are making food choices based on affordability is also borne out in the low frequency of purchases of protein-rich food items (fresh chicken, cooked chicken, cooked meat, dried fish, eggs, fresh fish, and fresh meat). The most common frequency of purchasing each of these food items was monthly. This is consistent with the low rates of consumption of meat, eggs, and fish reported in the Household Dietary Diversity Scores below.

## FIGURE 9: Reasons for Not Shopping at Supermarkets

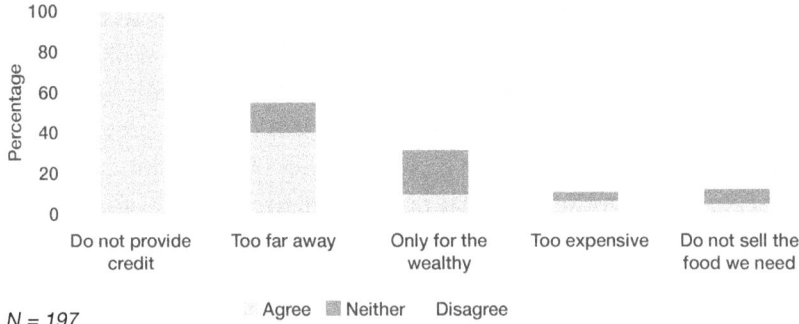

N = 197

Agree ■ Neither ▨ Disagree

## TABLE 5: Food Purchases by Frequency of Purchases

| | Purchased in the past month | | Frequency of purchase (of purchasing households) | | |
|---|---|---|---|---|---|
| | % Yes | % No | At least five days per week | At least once per week | At least once per month |
| Fresh vegetables | 100 | 0 | 58 | 40 | 2 |
| Chips, fried cassava or sweet potato | 100 | 0 | 20 | 57 | 23 |
| Sugar | 100 | 0 | 16 | 50 | 34 |
| Maize | 100 | 0 | 0 | 24 | 76 |
| Eggs | 100 | 0 | 0 | 8 | 92 |
| Fresh fish | 100 | 0 | 0 | 4 | 96 |
| Cooking oil | 97 | 3 | 24 | 53 | 20 |
| Cooked meat | 96 | 3 | 1 | 13 | 82 |
| Maize flour | 92 | 8 | 10 | 32 | 49 |
| Dried fish | 91 | 9 | 0 | 23 | 68 |
| Fresh chicken | 89 | 10 | 1 | 17 | 71 |
| Cooked chicken | 86 | 14 | 1 | 15 | 70 |
| Fresh fruit | 84 | 16 | 3 | 19 | 61 |
| Fresh meat | 83 | 17 | 0 | 2 | 81 |
| Rice | 80 | 20 | 9 | 21 | 49 |
| Bread | 28 | 72 | 2 | 8 | 18 |
| Fresh milk | 26 | 74 | 1 | 7 | 18 |

Fresh vegetables – widely available at markets, from mobile vendors, and at corner stalls in residential areas – were bought most frequently (Table 5). Nearly 60% of households purchased these at least five days per week, and almost all did so at least once per week. Cooking oil is the second most frequently purchased item. The oil is widely available in small plastic tubes (nicknamed "condoms") approximately one tablespoon in size, and many people who buy food on a daily basis buy these tubes at the same time. Ten percent of households purchase maize flour at least five days per week, with an additional 32% purchasing it weekly.

The frequent provisioning of maize flour contrasts with the conventional way of purchasing maize in whole-grain form in 50kg bags to consume over several weeks. Box 2 describes the origin of the term "walkman" to describe these small amounts of maize flour associated with economic precarity and food insecurity at the household level. Table 6 provides evidence that households that rely on daily purchases of maize flour are more food insecure than households that purchase maize flour less frequently. The mean HFIAS for households that purchase maize flour "at least 5 times per week" was 12.5, whereas the households that purchased maize flour less frequently had HFIAS scores ranging from 9.9-10.6, and the households that had not purchased maize flour in the past month had the lowest mean HFIAS score (9.6). All households purchased whole maize, but there was not a similar correlation between higher frequency of purchasing whole maize and higher HFIAS score (Table 6).

### TABLE 6: Food Security Status by Frequency of Purchasing Maize Flour/Whole Maize

|  | No. of households | Mean HFIAS |
|---|---|---|
| Maize flour | | |
| At least five days per week | 29 | 12.5 |
| At least once per week | 96 | 9.9 |
| At least twice per month | 109 | 10.0 |
| At least once per month | 37 | 10.6 |
| Did not purchase in the past month | 24 | 9.6 |
| Whole maize | | |
| At least once per week | 72 | 10.5 |
| At least twice per month | 70 | 9.6 |
| At least once per month | 153 | 10.5 |

## Box 2: The Origins of *Walkman* and the Increasing Precarity of Urban Households

Understanding food security in the Malawian context entails understanding the central importance of maize as a daily staple. While it is not a problem for urban Malawians to purchase the foods that accompany maize in a meal – relish – on a daily basis, the sense of "food security" in the home is bound up with having a large quantity of maize stored at home. During ethnographic research in Blantyre, Malawi, conducted in 2010, several respondents referred to daily purchases of maize flour - known colloquially as *walkman* – as evidence that they were experiencing food insecurity.[46] To be food secure was to buy a 50kg bag of maize and know that there would be staple food for the household for the next month or so. The term *walkman* originated in the 1990s when the eponymous personal music device was popular. People were embarrassed to be seen with these small quantities of maize flour because it signalled that their household did not have food, so they would pretend that it was a Walkman™ with a macabre sense of humour about the decline in urban living standards following structural adjustment reforms in the 1990s. Thus the signifier for a small purchase of maize or maize flour has outlived the device from which it took its name. In light of the local meaning of food security as having a large supply of maize in the home, which is linked to the agricultural experience of having a full granary, the popularity of the *walkman* is highly emblematic of the experience of urban food insecurity in Malawi. Even if people are managing to feed their households, they often go to bed wondering how they will eat the next day, or go to bed hungry because they have reserved some food in case of emergency.

Not all of the food consumed in urban households is purchased as many households produce some of their own food. Urban agriculture has been advanced as a key mitigator of urban food insecurity in the Southern African region by promoting self-reliance among low-income urban residents.[47] The 2008 AFSUN survey of households in low-income areas in 11 Southern African cities revealed extremely low rates of urban agriculture and far less than suggested by its advocates.[48] As Figure 10 shows, in eight of 11 cities, fewer than 30% of households procured food by producing it themselves. In over half of the cities, fewer than 10% were engaged in agriculture. Urban agriculture was almost non-existent in many informal settlements. One of the major exceptions to this regional pattern was Blantyre where over 60% of households were producing their own food.

The survey areas in Lilongwe were more like the urban environments where the other AFSUN surveys were conducted – high density, informal and low-income – and the findings were very similar. Only 10% of households in these areas of Lilongwe engage in urban agriculture (Table 4). The Lilongwe survey included questions about why households are not growing food (Figure 11). The respondents who were not involved in urban agriculture were presented with a set of possible factors influencing their decision and asked whether they agreed, disagreed, or were indifferent. The two main reasons were an absence of land on which to grow food (99% in agreement) and a lack of access to agricultural inputs (89% in agreement). Around one-quarter of the respondents agreed that it was easier to purchase food than grow it but the vast majority disagreed with statements like "we have no interest in growing food" and "farming is for rural people only." It appears, then, that the reasons for low rates of participation in urban agriculture are related more to an absence of means and resources than a lack of desire to produce food.

**FIGURE 10: Urban Agriculture in Southern African Cities**

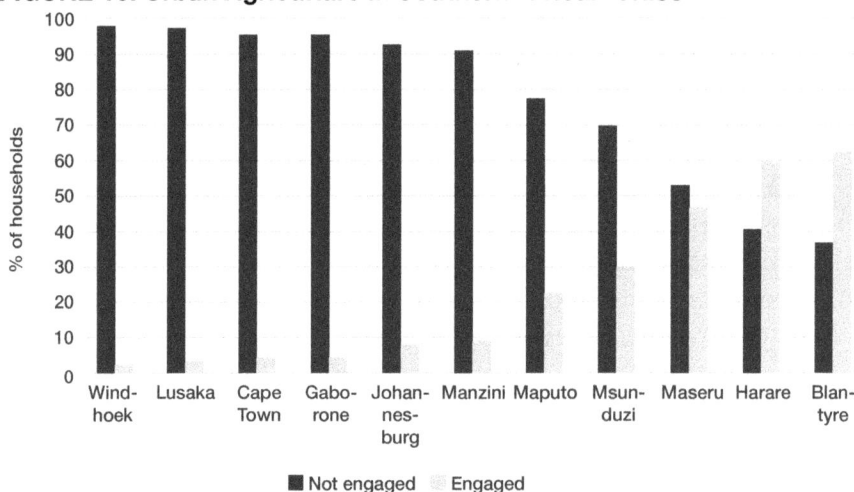

**FIGURE 11: Reasons for Not Growing Food**

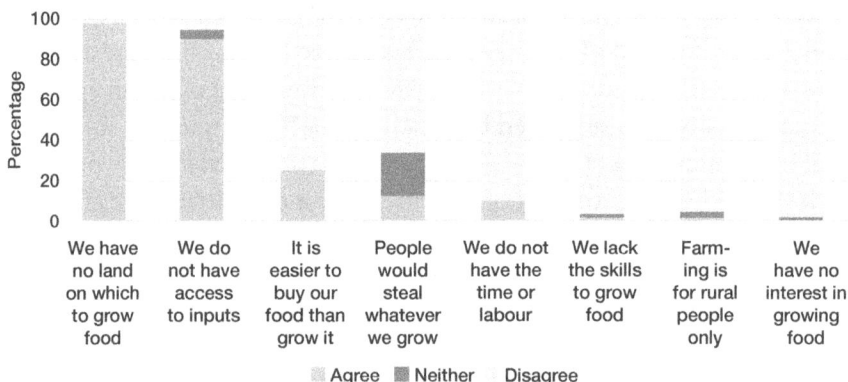

N = 259

# 6. HOUSEHOLD FOOD INSECURITY

The 2015 Lilongwe survey provides an opportunity to view previous AFSUN survey research in Malawi in a fresh light. The results of the food security status analysis are presented in Table 6, along with comparable figures from two sources: (a) the AFSUN baseline survey conducted in the peri-urban South Lunzu Ward in Blantyre City, and (b) the AFSUN baseline surveys conducted in low-income urban neighbourhoods in the cities of Gaborone, Windhoek, Lusaka, Maputo, Harare, Manzini, and Maseru. The comparisons are based on data collected at different times and therefore care must be exercised in their interpretation. For example, it is possible that conditions in Lilongwe's informal settlements were worse in 2015 than in 2008, when the other city surveys were done. However, the levels of food insecurity in the other SADC cities are so similar, and the differences with South Lunzu so dramatic, that some comparative commentary is justifiable.

| TABLE 7: Mean Food Security Scores in Low-Income Urban Neighbourhoods | | | |
|---|---|---|---|
| | Lilongwe 2015 | Blantyre (South Lunzu) 2008 | Other SADC cities 2008 |
| HFIAS | 10.3 | 5.3 | 12.2 |
| HFIAP | Food secure (%) | 3 | 34 | 7 |
| | Mildly food insecure (%) | 6 | 15 | 5 |
| | Moderately food insecure (%) | 19 | 30 | 22 |
| | Severely food insecure (%) | 72 | 21 | 67 |
| HDDS | 5.8 | 6.1 | 4.8 |
| MAHFP | 8.7 | 10.0 | 8.2 |
| Engagement in urban agriculture (%) | 10 | 62 | 25 |
| N | 300 | 432 | 3,409 |

South Lunzu in Blantyre had significantly lower levels of food insecurity, as measured by both the HFIAS and HFIAP, than the other seven SADC cities surveyed (Table 7). The mean HFIAS scores were 12.2 versus 5.3 (on a scale of 0 to 27 where food insecurity increases the higher the score). Only 7% of the households in the other SADC cities were food secure, while 67% were severely food insecure. The comparable figures for South Lunzu were 34% and 21%. These findings were a surprise since they suggested that Blantyre's urban poor were significantly more food secure than the urban poor in other comparable cities, especially given Malawi's relatively low development status.[49] However, they did pose the question of whether all of urban Malawi was similar to South Lunzu and, if not, whether more densely populated informal settlements were similar or different from peri-urban areas.

Table 7 makes it clear that informal settlements in Lilongwe are much more closely aligned with the other SADC cities than with South Lunzu in Blantyre. Lilongwe had a slightly better HFIAS score than the other SADC cities (10.3 versus 12.2), but on the HFIAP scale it had a higher rate of severely food insecure households (72% versus 67%) and a lower rate of food secure households (3% versus 7%). The higher food insecurity by HFIAP and lower food insecurity by HFIAS might suggest relatively high levels of inequality in Lilongwe, with some households with extremely favourable HFIAS scores lowering the average. However, this hypothesis is not borne out in the distribution of HFIAS scores presented in Table 8, which shows that at every interval of HFIAS score progression, Lilongwe has a higher percentage of households than the other SADC cities.

### TABLE 8: Distribution of HFIAS Scores in Low-Income Urban Neighbourhoods

| HFIAS score range | Cumulative % | | |
|---|---|---|---|
| | Lilongwe 2015 | Blantyre (South Lunzu) 2008 | Other SADC cities 2008 |
| 0-3 | 16 | 49 | 13 |
| 4-7 | 35 | 69 | 28 |
| 8-11 | 59 | 85 | 47 |
| 12-15 | 81 | 95 | 67 |
| 16-19 | 95 | 98 | 83 |
| 20-23 | 98 | 99 | 93 |
| 24-27 | 100 | 100 | 100 |

Another possible explanation for the worse HFIAP and better HFIAS results in Lilongwe is that household events considered "severe" in the HFIAP calculation are more widespread in that city, even among households that are less food insecure according to the HFIAS. A lower percentage of households in Lilongwe did report having the experiences in the first six HFIAS questions (Table 8) and these questions are considered less "severe" in HFIAP calculations. A greater percentage of households in Lilongwe also experienced the three most "severe" kinds of events. The widest gap was in having no food of any kind in the household due to a lack of resources; an event experienced by 59% of households in Lilongwe and 39% of households in the other SADC cities. This type of experience is characteristic of heightened precarity of incomes and of food sources. Thus, it seems that the food insecurity experience of households in Lilongwe is in the form of severe kinds of events.

Because food insecurity is a multifaceted phenomenon, it is best understood in relation to a range of food security metrics.[50] It is common to triangulate the HFIAS and HFIAP measures of food access with the HDDS measure of the quality of household diets. The HDDS measure of dietary diversity records how many food groups were consumed within the household in the previous 24 hours. The maximum number, based on the FAO classification of food groups for Africa, is 12. An increase in the average number of different food groups consumed provides a quantifiable measure of improved dietary diversity. In this regard, Lilongwe (5.8) was only slightly lower than Blantyre (6.1). The regional average for the other cities was 4.8; a figure lower than both sites in Malawi.

| TABLE 9: HFIAS Question Frequencies in Low-Income Urban Neighbourhoods | | | |
|---|---|---|---|
| | Percentage of households experiencing in past four weeks | | |
| | Lilongwe 2015 | Blantyre (South Lunzu) 2008 | Other SADC cities 2008 |
| Worry there would not be enough food | 77 | 46 | 80 |
| Not able to eat preferred food/lack of resources | 83 | 58 | 87 |
| Eat limited variety of food/lack of resources | 77 | 56 | 85 |
| Eat food you did not want to eat/lack of resources | 82 | 58 | 85 |
| Eat smaller meal than needed/lack of food | 73 | 39 | 79 |
| Eat fewer meals in a day/lack of food | 71 | 32 | 77 |
| No food of any kind to eat/lack of resources | 59 | 16 | 39 |
| Go to sleep at night hungry/lack of food | 52 | 17 | 46 |
| Go a whole day and night without eating anything/lack of food | 41 | 8 | 38 |

Table 10 provides details on what foods were being consumed, which helps interpret the nutritional significance of the diets in relation to the food security scores. Rates of consumption of the 12 food groups in the HDDS, ranked by the most to the least commonly consumed, in Lilongwe are shown along with the corresponding rates in Blantyre and other SADC cities. Turning first to the Lilongwe diet, the most widely consumed food group is foods made with grains; consumed by 94% of households in the previous 24 hours. This is consistent with the ubiquity of nsima made of maize at meal times. The majority also consumed vegetables (80%) and roots and tubers (63%). The bottom five foods are the most protein-rich foods: foods made from beans, peas, lentils, or nuts (39%); eggs (35%); fresh fish, dried fish or shellfish (32%); cheese, yoghurt, milk or other milk/dairy products (32%); and meat and other animal products (22%). This breakdown suggests that a narrow diversity in Lilongwe could be indicative of low consumption of the protein-rich foods required for a balanced and healthy diet.

**TABLE 10: Ranking of Food Groups from Most to Least Commonly Consumed**

| Rank-ing | Food group | % Consuming food group | | |
|---|---|---|---|---|
| | | Lilongwe 2015 | Blantyre (South Lunzu) 2008 | Other SADC cities 2008 |
| 1 | Any pasta, bread, rice noodles, biscuits or any other foods made from flour, millet, sorghum, maize, rice, wheat, or oats | 94 | 99 | 97 |
| 2 | Any other vegetables | 80 | 84 | 67 |
| 3 | Any potatoes, sweet potatoes, beetroot, carrots or any other foods made from them (e.g. chips, crisps) | 63 | 23 | 22 |
| 4 | Any other foods, such as condi-ments, coffee, tea | 50 | 87 | 56 |
| 5 | Any sugar or honey (including sugar in tea, coffee etc) | 49 | 84 | 57 |
| 6 | Any foods made with oil, fat, or butter | 45 | 54 | 50 |
| 7 | Any fruits | 39 | 43 | 24 |
| 8 | Any foods made from beans, peas, lentils, or nuts | 39 | 31 | 19 |
| 9 | Eggs | 35 | 16 | 17 |
| 10 | Any fresh fish, dried fish, or shellfish | 32 | 45 | 17 |
| 11 | Any cheese, yoghurt, milk, or other milk/dairy products | 32 | 18 | 21 |
| 12 | Any beef, pork, lamb, goat, rab-bit, wild game, chicken, duck, other birds, chicken heads and feet, liver, kidney, heart, or other organ meats/offal or products | 22 | 23 | 37 |

A comparison of the 2015 Lilongwe data with that from the other SADC cities and Blantyre in 2008 highlights some differences that could be the basis for conjecture about the changing food systems in low-income urban neighbourhoods in Southern Africa. The percentage of households consuming potatoes and related foods, including chips, is much higher in Lilongwe (63%) compared to both Blantyre (23%) and other SADC cities (22%). One plausible explanation could be the wider availability and affordability of chips in 2015, which would be consistent with the "nutrition transition" trend observed in African cities.[51] Another plausible explanation is linked to the lower consumption of grains and the poor maize harvest in 2015; sweet potatoes and other tubers are often consumed as a substitute when maize is unavailable or inaccessible.[52] Without further follow-up questions it is not clear if people are eating foods from this group out of choice or necessity.

In Lilongwe in 2015, there was a noticeably higher rate of consumption of eggs and dairy products relative to the 2008 surveys. These changes could also point to a changing food system, particularly in the case of dairy products that require processing. On the other hand, the rate of consumption of meat, which is emblematic of urbanizing diets, was lowest in Lilongwe (22%). This could be due to the Malawian context rather than indicative of regional trends as the rate of consumption of meat in Blantyre (at 23%) was similar to the rate in Lilongwe and far below the rate in the other SADC cities (at 37%). In both Malawi surveys, rates of consumption of fish and beans were higher than for the other cities in the region. While Table 10 does not provide directly comparable case study evidence that could demonstrate changing urban diets in the region, it does show some interesting patterns that raise further questions.

The final food security measure, the MAHFP indicator, captures changes in the household's ability to ensure that food is available throughout the year. Households are asked to identify in which months (during the past 12) they did not have access to sufficient food to meet their household needs. Lilongwe had an average score of 8.7, compared to 10.0 in Blantyre and 8.2 in the other cities. A higher score suggests more consistent access to food over the course of a year. Figure 12 illustrates the distribution of MAHFP scores in Lilongwe. Only 9% of households had a score of 12, meaning that they had adequate food in all 12 months. More than half (52%) of households had scores of 7 or 8. These findings suggest that seasonal fluctuations in food access are widespread. The month-by-month breakdown in Figure 13 suggests a strong correlation between the agricultural cycle and the times in the year when the urban poor in Lilongwe have constrained access to food. January, February and March are known as the "hungry season" as they fall just before the maize harvest. This is when food supplies are lowest and the prices are often higher.[53]

The size of the harvest in the year of the survey could be a contributing factor in the wide difference between the results in Blantyre in 2008 and Lilongwe in 2015. The year 2008 had bumper maize harvests due in part to the roll out of a popular fertilizer subsidy programme, whereas 2015 had a weak maize harvest for reasons noted above.[54,55] Another factor is the geographical difference between the areas surveyed. Nearly two-thirds of households in South Lunzu, Blantyre, produced some of their own food because they were located in a peri-urban area where land was available for cultivation.[56] Moreover, the customary land system meant that many low-income households had access to farmland near their homes.[57] During in-depth interviews conducted in 2010, some urban households said that they received fertilizer coupons either because their "home village" was located in the city or because of close ties with their rural "home village" even though urban residents were technically excluded from the programme.[58] In Lilongwe, however, the high density of the settlement, the insecurity of tenure for most residents, and the high cost of rented farmland, all contribute to a land shortage that largely explains the low rate of participation in urban agriculture.

**FIGURE 12: Months of Adequate Household Food Provisioning (% of Households)**

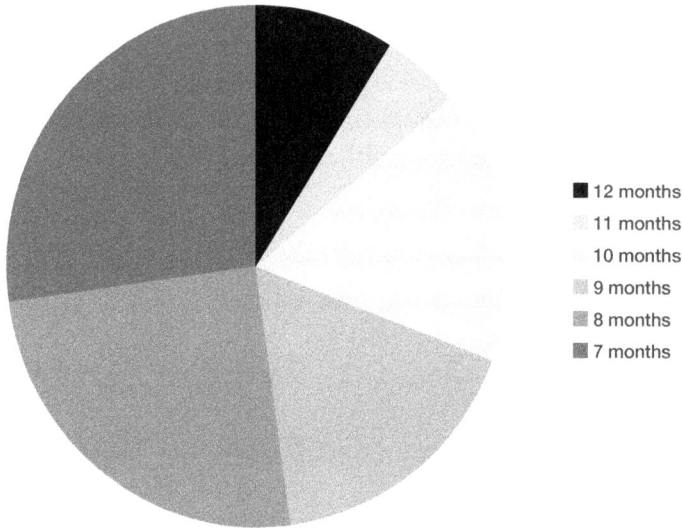

- 12 months
- 11 months
- 10 months
- 9 months
- 8 months
- 7 months

**FIGURE 13: Percentage of Households with Adequate Food by Month**

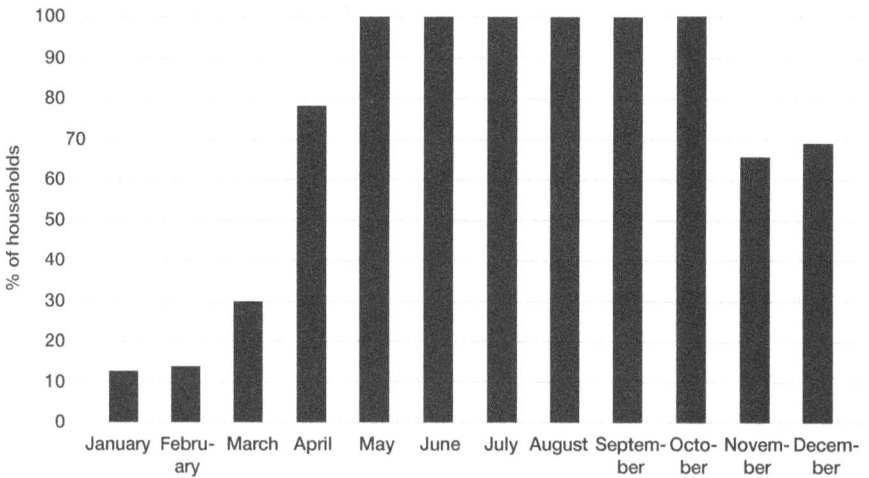

# 7. CONCLUSION

The Lilongwe survey contributes an added dimension to the body of research initiated by AFSUN, by addressing the apparent anomaly that levels of food security were higher in Malawi (Blantyre) than in virtually every other SADC city surveyed. This counter-intuitive finding was largely because the type of peri-urban area surveyed in Blantyre differed from that in most other cities. The unresolved question was whether there were intra-urban differences in Malawi and whether the country's informal settlements were similar to peri-urban areas or more like other informal settlements throughout the region. The findings discussed here provide a complementary perspective to the 2008 AFSUN survey, which suggested a level of food security in urban Malawi that was probably more typical of peri-urban areas where many people farm and was done in a year when there was a bumper maize harvest.

Given that informal settlements house the majority of the country's urban residents and the lion's share of new migrants to Lilongwe, the research presents a serious public policy challenge for Malawi's leaders. The picture that emerges is that Malawi's urban communities are internally diverse and that urban poverty is a profound problem in Malawi's rapidly expanding cities. Of particular note is the poor quality of diets in these communities where protein deficiency should receive additional research attention.

The precarity of income, reflected in the frequent purchasing of staple foods and the need for food sellers to extend credit, appears to be a key driver of food insecurity in these communities. Given that lack of land was the main reason for not practising urban agriculture, it does not seem to be a feasible policy option to provide farmland to poor residents in the sprawling city. The positive correlation between urban agriculture and food security in South Lunzu, Blantyre, seems to be related to a set of contextual factors that cannot practically be replicated in Lilongwe's informal settlements. Economically inclusive growth, with better prospects for stable employment and protection for informal-sector workers, appears to be the surest route to improved food security.

# ENDNOTES

1      Crush and Battersby, *Rapid Urbanisation, Urban Food Deserts and Food Security in Africa*; Crush and Frayne, "Feeding African Cities."

2      Mvula and Chiweza, *The State of Food Insecurity in Blantyre, Malawi.*

3      Manda, *Situation of Urbanisation in Malawi Report.*

4      UNHABITAT, *Malawi: Lilongwe Urban Profile*, p. 7.

5      Ibid.

6      World Bank, *Malawi Urbanization Review.*

7      IOM, *Migration in Malawi: Country Profile*; Johnson, "After the Mines"; Potts, "Rural Mobility as a Response to Land Shortages."

8      Riley and Dodson, "Gendered Mobilities and Food Access in Blantyre, Malawi."

9      World Bank, *Malawi Urbanization Review.*

10      Riley, "Operation *Dongosolo* and the Geographies of Urban Poverty in Malawi."

11      Englund, "The Village in the City, the City in the Village."

12      Peters, "Rural Income and Poverty in a Time of Radical Change in Malawi"; Takane, *Current Issues of Rural Development in Malawi.*

13      Lerner and Eakin, "An Obsolete Dichotomy?"; Agergaard et al., *Rural-Urban Dynamics.*

14      Mkwambisi et al., "Urban Agriculture and Poverty Reduction."

15      Harris et al., *Mapping the Linkages Between Agriculture, Food Security and Nutrition in Malawi.*

16      Bezner Kerr, "Lost and Found Crops."

17      Potts, "Challenging the Myths of Urban Dynamics in Sub-Saharan Africa."

18      Suckall at al., "Reduced Migration Under Climate Change"; Suckall et al., "Using a Migration Systems Approach to Understand the Link between Climate Change and Urbanisation in Malawi."

19      Ibid.

20      Hoornweg and Pope, "Population Predictions for the World's Largest Cities."

21      Kalipeni, "Spatial Context of Lilongwe's Growth and Development"; Potts, "Capital Relocation in Africa."

22      Chilowa, *Food Insecurity and Coping Strategies.*

23      Mambo, "Perilous Connections."

24      Frayne et al., *State of Urban Food Insecurity in Southern Africa.*

25      Headey and Ecker, "Rethinking the Measurement of Food Security; Coates et al., "Household Food Insecurity Access Scale".

26      Vilili et al., *'Operation of the Market' Study.*

27      Chipeta and Kachaka, *Role of Migrants' Remittances.*

28      Brooks and Loftus, "Africa's Passive Revolution"; Zimmerman, "Voter Response to Scandal"; Kayuni "Running to Stand Still."

29      Riley and Chilanga, "'Cashgate Has Compromised Our Livelihoods."

30      Government of Malawi, *Malawi 2015 Floods.*

31    World Bank Group, United Nations, and the European Union, *Malawi Drought 2015-2016.*

32    Ibid.

33    Ibid., p. 3.

34    Crush and Frayne, "Supermarket Expansion and the Informal Food Economy."

35    Peyton et al., "Implications of Supermarket Expansion."

36    Madziakapita, "Situational Analysis of the Informal Sector"; Power "'Eating the Property."

37    Jimu, "Negotiated Economic Opportunity and Power."

38    The funds were redirected from the Press Trust, a trust set up for public works project from wealth accumulated by Life President Kamuzu Banda through the Malawi Congress Party's economic influence under the one-party system; see Riley, "Operation *Dongosolo.*"

39    Riley, "Operation *Dongosolo*"; Tonda and Kepe, "Spaces of Contention."

40    Cammack, "Malawi in Crisis, 2011-12."

41    Crush and Frayne, "Supermarket Expansion"

42    Crush and Battersby, "Rapid Urbanization."

43    De Groote and Kimenju, "Comparing Consumer Preferences for Color and Nutritional Quality in Maize"; Legwegoh and Hovorka, "Exploring Food Choices Within the Context of Nutritional Security in Gaborone"; Riley and Dodson, "Intersectional Identities."

44    For details about the history of food retailing in Malawi see van Donge, "Fate of an African 'Chaebol'"; Chihana, "Urbanization and Food Production and Marketing"; Power, "Race, Class, Ethnicity, and Anglo-Indian Trade Rivalry."

45    See http://spar-international.com/country/malawi/

46    Riley, "Gendered Geographies of Food Security in Blantyre."

47    Redwood, *Agriculture in Urban Planning*; Mougeot, *Agropolis.*

48    Frayne et al., "Mythology of Urban Agriculture"; Crush et al., "Food Security in Southern African Cities."

49    Mvula and Chiweza, *Food Insecurity in Blantyre.*

50    Headey and Ecker, "Rethinking the Measurement of Food Security."

51    Nnyepi et al., "Evidence of Nutrition Transition in Southern Africa"; De Groote and Kimenju "Comparing Consumer Preferences."

52    The preference for maize has been a contentious issue in food policy debates, particularly in relation to the role of Malawians' inflexible food preference for maize even when cassava and sweet potatoes were available during the 2001-02 famine; see Devereux, *State of Disaster.*

53    Aberman et al., *Mapping the Linkages.*

54    Chirwa and Chinsinga, "Political Economy of Food Price Policy in Malawi."

55    FEWSNET, *Malawi Food Security Outlook.*

56    Mvula and Chiweza, *Food Insecurity in Blantyre.*

57    Riley and Legwegoh, "Comparative Urban Food Geographies."

58    Riley, "Gendered Geographies of Food Security."

# REFERENCES

1.  Aberman, N., Meerman, J. and Benson, T. eds. (2015). *Mapping the Linkages Between Agriculture, Food Security and Nutrition in Malawi.* Washington, DC: IFPRI.

2.  Agergaard, J., Fold, N. and Gough, K., eds. (2010). *Rural-Urban Dynamics: Livelihoods, Mobility and Markets in African and Asian Frontiers.* New York: Routledge.

3.  Bezner Kerr, R. (2014). "Lost and Found Crops: Agrobiodiversity, Indigenous Knowledge, and a Feminist Political Ecology of Sorghum and Finger Millet in Northern Malawi" *Annals of the Association of American Geographers* 104: 577-593.

4.  Brooks, A. and Loftus, A. (2016). "Africa's Passive Revolution: Crisis in Malawi." *Transactions of the Institute of British Geographers* 41: 258-272.

5.  Cammack, D. (2012). "Malawi in Crisis, 2011-12" *Review of African Political Economy* 39: 375-388.

6.  Chihana, H. (1994). "Urbanization and Food Production and Marketing: The Case of Lunzu Market Area in Blantyre, 1895-1964" *The Society of Malawi Journal* 47: 1-31.

7.  Chilowa, W. (1991). *Food Insecurity and Coping Strategies Among the Low Income Urban Households in Malawi.* Bergen: Chr Michelson Institute.

8.  Chipeta, C. and Kachaka, W. (2005) *Role of Migrants' Remittances in an Unstable Low-Income Economy: A Case Study of Malawi. Department of Economics Working Paper 2005/05.* Zomba: University of Malawi.

9.  Chirwa, E. and Chinsinga, B. (2015). "The Political Economy of Food Price Policy in Malawi" In P. Pinstrup-Anderson, ed., *Food Price Policy in an Era of Market Instability: A Political Economy Analysis.* Oxford: Oxford University Press, pp. 154-173.

10. Coates, J., Swindale, A. and Bilinsky, P. (2007). *Household Food Insecurity Access Scale (HFIAS) for Measurement of Household Food Access: Indicator Guide (Version 3). Food and Nutrition Technical Assistance Project.* Washington, DC: Academy for Educational Development.

11. Crush, J. and Battersby, J., eds., *Rapid Urbanisation, Urban Food Deserts and Food Security in Africa*. Cham, Switzerland: Springer.

12. Crush, J. and Frayne, B. (2014). "Feeding African Cities: The Growing Challenge of Urban Food Insecurity" In S. Parnell and E. Pieterse, eds., *Africa's Urban Revolution*. London: Zed Books, pp. 110-132.

13. Crush, J. and Frayne, B. (2011). "Supermarket Expansion and the Informal Food Economy in Southern African Cities: Implications for Urban Food Security" *Journal of Southern African Studies* 37: 781-807.

14. Crush, J., Hovorka, A. and Tevera, D. (2011). "Food Security in Southern African Cities: The Place of Urban Agriculture" *Progress in Development Studies* 11: 285-305.

15. De Groote, H. and Kimenju, S. (2008). "Comparing Consumer Preferences for Color and Nutritional Quality in Maize: Application of a Semi-Double-Bound Logistic Model on Urban Consumers in Kenya" *Food Policy*, 33: 362-370.

16. Devereux, S. (2002). *State of Disaster: Causes, Consequences & Policy Lessons from Malawi*. Lilongwe: Actionaid.

17. Dodson, B., Chiweza, A. and Riley, L. (2012). *Gender and Food Insecurity in Southern African Cities*. Cape Town: African Food Security Urban Network.

18. Englund, H. (2001). "The Village in the City, the City in the Village: Migrants in Lilongwe" *Journal of Southern African Studies* 28: 137-154.

19. FEWSNET (2015). *Malawi Food Security Outlook: High Prices, Declining Incomes, and Poor Winter Production Cause Crisis Food Insecurity* Lilongwe: USAID.

20. Frayne, B. et al. (2010). *The State of Urban Food Insecurity in Southern Africa*. Cape Town: African Food Security Urban Network.

21. Frayne, B., McCordic, C. and Shilomboleni, H. (2016). "The Mythology of Urban Agriculture" In J. Crush and J. Battersby, eds., *Rapid Urbanisation, Urban Food Deserts and Food Insecurity in Africa*. Cham, Switzerland: Springer, pp. 19-32.

22. Government of Malawi (2015). *Malawi 2015 Floods Post Disaster Needs*

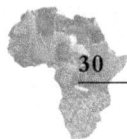

*Assessment Report.* Lilongwe: Government of Malawi, the World Bank, the UN, and the EU.

23. Government of Malawi (2010). *Projections of Population Growth to 2050.* Zomba: Malawi National Statistics Office.

24. Harris, J., Meerman, J. and Aberman, N., eds. (2015) *Mapping the Linkages Between Agriculture, Food Security and Nutrition in Malawi.* Washington, DC: IFPRI.

25. Headey, D. and Ecker, O. (2013). "Rethinking the Measurement of Food Security: From First Principles to Best Practice" *Food Security* 5: 327-343.

26. Hoornweg, D. and Pope, K. (2017). "Population Predictions for the World's Largest Cities in the 21st Century" *Environment & Urbanization* 29: 195–216.

27. International Organization for Migration (2014). *Migration in Malawi: Country Profile.* Geneva: IOM.

28. Jimu, I. (2005). "Negotiated Economic Opportunity and Power: Perspectives and Perceptions of Street Vending in Urban Malawi" *African Development* 30: 35-51.

29. Johnson, J. (2017). "After the Mines: The Changing Social and Economic Landscape of Malawi–South Africa Migration" *Review of African Political Economy* 44: 237-251.

30. Kalipeni, E. (1999). "The Spatial Context of Lilongwe's Growth and Development" In P. Zeleza and E. Kalipeni, eds., *Sacred Spaces and Public Quarrels: African Cultural and Economic Landscapes* Trenton, NJ: Africa World Press, pp. 73-110.

31. Kayuni, S. (2016). "Running to Stand Still: Reflections on the Cashgate Scandal Heist in Malawi" *Journal of Money Laundering Control*, 19: 169-188.

32. Legwegoh, A. and Hovorka, A. (2016). "Exploring Food Choices Within the Context of Nutritional Security in Gaborone, Botswana" *Singapore Journal of Tropical Geography* 37: 76-93.

33. Lerner, A. and Eakin, H. (2011). "An Obsolete Dichotomy? Rethinking the Rural-Urban Interface in Terms of Food Security and Production in the Global South" *The Geographic Journal* 177: 311-320.

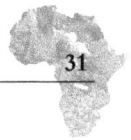

34. Madziakapita, S. (2009). "A Situational Analysis of the Informal Sector in the Three Major Cities (Blantyre, Lilongwe and Mzuzu) of Malawi" PhD Thesis, University of South Africa, Pretoria.

35. Mambo, T. (2016). "Perilous Connections: Poverty, Food Insecurity, HIV/AIDS, and Gender in Lilongwe, Malawi" PhD Thesis, University of Calgary, Calgary.

36. Manda, M. (2013). *Situation of Urbanisation in Malawi Report*. Lilongwe: Government of Malawi Ministry of Lands and Housing.

37. Mkwambisi, D., Fraser, E. and Dougill, A. (2011). "Urban Agriculture and Poverty Reduction: Evaluating How Food Production in Cities Contributes to Food Security, Employment and Income in Malawi" *Journal of International Development* 23: 181-203.

38. Mougeot, L., ed. (2005). *Agropolis: The Social, Political and Environmental Dimensions of Urban Agriculture*. Ottawa: IDRC.

39. Nnyepi, N. Gwisai, N., Lekgoa, M. and Seru, T. (2015). "Evidence of Nutrition Transition in Southern Africa" *Proceedings of the Nutrition Society*, 74: 478-486.

40. Peters, P. (2006). "Rural Income and Poverty in a Time of Radical Change in Malawi" *Journal of Development Studies* 42: 322-345.

41. Peyton, S., Moseley, W., and Battersby, J. (2015). "Implications of Supermarket Expansion on Urban Food Security in Cape Town, South Africa" *African Geographical Review* 34: 36-54.

42. Potts, D. (2012). "Challenging the Myths of Urban Dynamics in Sub-Saharan Africa: The Evidence from Nigeria" *World Development* 40: 1382-1393.

43. Potts, D. (2006). "Rural Mobility as a Response to Land Shortages: The Case of Malawi" *Population, Space and Place* 12: 291-311.

44. Potts, D. (1985). "Capital Relocation in Africa: The Case of Lilongwe in Malawi" *The Geographical Journal* 151: 182-196.

45. Power, J. (1995). "'Eating the Property:' Gender Roles and Economic Change in Urban Malawi, Blantyre-Limbe, 1907-1953" *Canadian Journal of African Studies* 29: 79-107.

46. Power, J. (1993). "Race, Class, Ethnicity, and Anglo-Indian Trade

Rivalry in Colonial Malawi, 1910-1945" *The International Journal of African Historical Studies* 26: 575-607.

47. Redwood, M., ed. (2008). *Agriculture in Urban Planning: Generating Livelihoods and Food Security*. Ottawa: IDRC.

48. Riley, L. (2014). "Operation Dongosolo and the Geographies of Urban Poverty in Malawi" *Journal of Southern African Studies* 40: 443-458.

49. Riley, L. (2013). "Gendered Geographies of Food Security in Blantyre, Malawi" PhD Thesis, University of Western Ontario, London (Canada).

50. Riley, L. and Chilanga, E. (2016). "'Cashgate Has Compromised Our Livelihoods:' Popular Politics of Food Security in Lilongwe's Informal Settlements" Paper presented at Canadian Association of African Studies Conference, University of Calgary, Calgary.

51. Riley, L. and Dodson, B. (2017). "Intersectional Identities: Food, Space and Gender in Urban Malawi" *Agenda: Empowering Women for Gender Equity* 30: 53-61.

52. Riley, L. and Dodson, B. (2014). "Gendered Mobilities and Food Access in Blantyre, Malawi" *Urban Forum* 25: 227-239.

53. Riley, L. and Legwegoh, A. (2014). "Comparative Urban Food Geographies in Blantyre and Gaborone" *African Geographical Review* 33: 52-66.

54. Spar (2017). "Spar Malawi." Online. http://spar-international.com/country/malawi/

55. Suckall, N., Fraser, E., Forster, P. and Mkwambisi, D. (2015). "Using a Migration Systems Approach to Understand the Link between Climate Change and Urbanisation in Malawi" *Applied Geography* 63: 244-252.

56. Takane, T., ed. (2006). *Current Issues of Rural Development in Malawi. Africa Research Series Number 12*. Chiba: Institute for Developing Economies.

57. Tonda, N. and Kepe, T. (2016). "Spaces of Contention: Tension Around Street Vendors' Struggle for Livelihoods and Spatial Justice in Lilongwe, Malawi" *Urban Forum* 27: 297-309.

58. UNHABITAT (2011) *Malawi: Lilongwe Urban Profile*. Nairobi: UNHABITAT.

59. Van Donge, J. (2002). "The Fate of an African 'Chaebol': Malawi's Press Corporation after Democratization" *Journal of Modern African Studies* 40: 651-681.

60. Vilili, G., Rain-Taljaard, R., Monkwe, C., Tsepe, M. and Gordon, R. (2013). *'Operation of the Market' Study: How the Poor Access, Hold and Trade Land: Findings from Research in Two Settlements in Lilongwe, Malawi.* Lilongwe: CCODE and Malawi Homeless People's Federation.

61. World Bank (2016). *Republic of Malawi: Malawi Urbanization Review: Leveraging Urbanization for National Growth and Development.* Washington, DC: World Bank.

62. World Bank Group, United Nations, and the European Union (2016). *Malawi Drought 2015-2016: Post-Disaster Needs Assessment.* Washington, DC: World Bank.

63. Zimmerman, B. (2015). "Voter Response to Scandal: Cashgate" In N. Patel and M. Wahman, eds., *The Malawi 2014 Tripartite Elections: Is Democracy Maturing?* Lilongwe: National Initiative for Civic Education, pp. 215-235.

www.ingramcontent.com/pod-product-compliance
Lightning Source LLC
Chambersburg PA
CBHW080135270326
41926CB00021B/4490